WHEN I PRAY
31 Days of Wisdom for Women
From the Book of Psalms

Kristy Marcotte

STFW Press

LADERA RANCH, CALIFORNIA

Copyright © 2016 by **Kristy Marcotte**

All rights reserved. No part of this publication may be reproduced, distributed or transmitted in any form or by any means, including photocopying, recording, or other electronic or mechanical methods, without the prior written permission of the publisher, except in the case of brief quotations embodied in critical reviews and certain other non-commercial uses permitted by copyright law. For permission requests, write to the publisher, addressed "Attention: Permissions Coordinator," at the address below:

STFW Press
27702 Crown Valley Pkwy D-4
#134
Ladera Ranch, CA 92694
www.KristyMarcotte.com

Scripture quotations marked (NIV) are taken from the Holy Bible, New International Version®, NIV®. Copyright © 1973, 1978, 1984, 2011 by Biblica, Inc.™ Used by permission of Zondervan. All rights reserved worldwide. www.zondervan.com The "NIV" and "New International Version" are trademarks registered in the United States Patent and Trademark Office by Biblica, Inc.™

Scripture quotations marked (NLT) are taken from the Holy Bible, New Living Translation, copyright ©1996, 2004, 2007, 2013 by Tyndale House Foundation. Used by permission of Tyndale House Publishers, Inc., Carol Stream, Illinois 60188. All rights reserved.Book Layout © 2014 BookDesignTemplates.com

When I Pray - 31 Days of Wisdom for Women From the Book of Psalms / Kristy Marcotte -- 1st ed.
ISBN 978-0-9984079-1-3

CONTENTS

Introduction 1
Day 1: Wisdom for Clear Instructions 3
Day 2: Wisdom for Taking Action 7
Day 3: Wisdom for Overcoming Guilt 9
Day 4: Wisdom for When I Need Patience 11
Day 5: Wisdom for Direction 15
Day 6: Wisdom for Growing a Strong Faith 17
Day 7: Wisdom for When I Need a Thankful Heart 19
Day 8: Wisdom for Defeating Worry 21
Day 9: Wisdom for Building Trust 25
Day 10: Wisdom for When I Lose My Focus 27
Day 11: Wisdom for Becoming Wise 29
Day 12: Wisdom for Gaining Control of My Mouth 33
Day 13: Wisdom for Choosing the Right Path 37
Day 14: Wisdom for When I Want to Give Up on Someone 39
Day 15: Wisdom for Learning to be Humble 43
Day 16: Wisdom for Living a Prosperous Life 45
Day 17: Wisdom for Escaping the Traps of My Enemies 49
Day 18: Wisdom for Eliminating Distractions 53
Day 19: Wisdom for Handling Criticism 57
Day 20: Wisdom for What to Do When I Must Wait 59

Day 21: Wisdom for When I'm Paralyzed by Indecision.............. 63
Day 22: Wisdom for Understanding God's Power........................ 65
Day 23: Wisdom for When I'm Out of DIY Strength 69
Day 24: Wisdom for Stepping Out in Faith................................... 73
Day 25: Wisdom for Being a Good Follower............................... 75
Day 26: Wisdom for When a Situation is Out of My Control....... 79
Day 27: Wisdom for Saying "Yes" to God's Best 83
Day 28: Wisdom for Getting Through Times of Famine 87
Day 29: Wisdom for Overcoming Fearful Thoughts.................... 89
Day 30: Wisdom for Choosing Helpful & Truthful Words........... 93
Day 31: Wisdom for Defeating Hopelessness............................... 97

INTRODUCTION

Introduction

It is not an accident that you are reading this book. Accidents are not part of God's vocabulary. There is power when you pray. So, my prayer is that you will get to the end of the next 31 days knowing God more deeply and living life more passionately.

I have neatly packaged this book into 31 daily devotions. There is a verse from the Book of Psalms, a note from me, and a prayer to pray for each day of the month.

You're going to need a journal or something to write your thoughts in. If you don't have a journal, I have created journal pages you can download and use. Download them by going to my website: www.straighttalkforwomen.com.

Are you ready? Sit down, buckle up, and prepare to be encouraged and motivated every day for the next 31 days!

- Kristy Marcotte

PSALMS 1:1-3

Day 1: Wisdom for Clear Instructions

"Oh, the joys of those who do not follow the advice of the wicked, or stand around with sinners, or join in with mockers. But they delight in the law of the Lord, meditating on it day and night. They are like trees planted along the riverbank, bearing fruit each season. Their leaves never wither, and they prosper in all they do."
Psalms 1:1-3 (NLT)

I bought a coffee table recently, and when I went to assemble it, I found the instruction manual was compiled of only pictures. There were no written instructions. I had to look at the picture and then guess what the manufacturer wanted me to do with the pieces. I was beyond aggravated. Really? We've resorted to pictures only? Needless to say, even with both my husband and I putting the table together, we had a really tough go with it.

I'm really glad God didn't give us a book full of pictures to guess what to do. Psalms 1:1-3 is clear.

Those who do these four things:

1. Don't follow the advice of the wicked
2. Don't stand around with sinners
3. Don't join in with mockers
4. Delight in the law of the Lord meditating on it day and night

They can expect to:

1. Have joy
2. Be strong like trees planted along the riverbank
3. Be consistently productive like trees that bear fruit each season
4. Prosper in ALL they do

So ask yourself, "How am I doing in these four areas?" To whom am I going for advice? With whom am I hanging around? Am I being critical or judgmental of someone right now?

Perhaps, if you focus steadily on the fourth area; "Delight in the law of the Lord meditating on it day and night," the first three will probably become non issues.

I challenge you to work on these four areas starting today! If you're tech savvy, download the YouVersion Bible app and highlight this group of verses. Read them over and over every time you pick up your cell phone; that shouldn't be hard. Some of us hardly set down our phones. LOL. If you would like, look me up and become "friends" with me on the Bible app!

Another idea is to take a picture of the verse in your Bible with your cell phone and then save it as your background. If downloading apps on your cell phone seems like too much trouble; go old school. Write down the verses on a 3x5 index card and keep it in your purse to pull out and read anytime throughout the day.

If you truly want to see real lasting change in your life; it's go time, girl! Get yourself a journal, if you don't already have one. Write this verse in it and spend time reflecting on it. Of course, you can download my free journal pages as well by going to my website: www.straighttalkforwomen.com.

Today's Prayer:

Lord, I am so thankful that Your instructions in Psalms 1:1-3 are very clear. Lord, I want to have joy, be strong, and prosper in everything I do, so I ask You to change me as I start applying these verses in my life over these next 31 days. Help me to avoid those who are a bad influence on me. Reveal to me anyone I need to distance myself from right now. Lord, help me to carve out time every day to be with You and meditate on Your word. In Jesus' name, I pray, AMEN.

PSALM 2:8

Day 2:
Wisdom for Taking Action

"Only ask, and I will give you the nations as your inheritance, the whole earth as your possession."
Psalm 2:8 (NLT)

Whenever you get tempted to think, why pray today. God's probably not listening or just too busy anyway…think again.

He wants us to ask Him for whatever we need. Just picture Him standing in front of you with His arms stretched out while saying, "If you will just ask me, my child. I really want to help you! Just ask!"

More often the problem is not that God is too busy: it's we who are too busy. We try to handle everything all by ourselves. I challenge you to just ask God to help you with that problem you're trying to fix on your own. Be specific.

For example, don't just pray for His help to make you a better person. Pray for His help to get you up a little extra early tomorrow morning and every morning for the next 31 days so you can spend the first part of your day with Him.

In fact, take action and make a commitment today to go to bed a little earlier so you can spend at least 15 minutes every morning with God. He is waiting for you to go to Him with all your needs. Are you ready to ask?

Write this verse in your journal and then right below start with your first request. You've got to start somewhere, right? Do it now.

Today's Prayer:

Lord, You tell us in Psalm 2:8 to ask and You will give us the nations as our inheritance, the whole earth as our possession…so today I'm going to take action and start asking! First, help me to put You first in my day. Help me get up a little earlier every day to meet with You. I also need help with (fill in the blank). I ask for Your help with all these things. In Jesus' name, I pray, AMEN.

PSALM 4:1

Day 3:
Wisdom for Overcoming Guilt

"Answer me when I call to You, O God who declares me innocent. Free me from my troubles. Have mercy on me and hear my prayer."
Psalm 4:1 (NLT)

When I first read this verse, the part I choked on was *"...O God who declares me innocent."* I have a hard time really feeling innocent inside. I tend to jump to the *"...Free me from my troubles. Have mercy on me and hear my prayer..."* part. Now that part of the verse I can identify with very easily. But the *God declaring me innocent* part, not so much. I know myself pretty well, and, well, "innocent" isn't usually my first thought.

Do you feel this way too sometimes? It's easy to see ourselves as the sinners we've always been instead of the saved ones that Jesus has made us. I encourage you to remember that because of what Jesus did for us on the cross, not just some of our sins, but ALL of our sins have been forgiven. Yep, even the ones you and I will do later today.

Pray out to God today. See Him as the God who declares you innocent, not the God who is waiting to judge you. Thank Him for giving His only son to die on the cross to pay for your sins so that you could be declared innocent.

As you meditate on this verse, ask yourself, "Do I feel like God has declared me innocent? Or do I feel like He's just waiting to punish me?" Which of these questions makes you want to be closer to God? Naturally, we want to be closer to someone who sees us as innocent, right?

This is the kind of God we have! A God who sees us as innocent! His son paid the price. So stop beating yourself up. If God has declared you innocent; stop listening to the condemnation of the enemy. Whatever your troubles are today, go to God boldly. Ask Him to fill you with the strength you need to do whatever it is you need to do.

Today's Prayer:

Lord, thank You so much for answering when I call on You for help. Thank You for forgiving me and declaring me innocent. Please help me to see when I am beating myself up and allowing negative thoughts to drag me down and hold me captive! In Jesus' name, I pray, AMEN.

PSALM 5:3

Day 4:
Wisdom for When I Need Patience

"Listen to my voice in the morning, Lord. Each morning I bring my requests to You and wait expectantly."
Psalm 5:3 (NLT)

I like to pray to God in the morning. In fact, I love even writing out my prayers in a journal. I first write the things for which I'm thankful. Next I start in on my long laundry list of requests. Then, I close my journal and run, literally, upstairs to get ready for work. It's kind of like...*checked that off the list*. Now, I'll go get busy with other things and come back tomorrow morning to see if any of my prayers were answered.

This scenario reminds me of when I went fishing at my grandparents' lake when I was little. I would hurry up and stick that squirmy little worm on my fishing pole, cast it out into the lake, stick my pole into a nearby hole in the ground, and run off to play. A few hours later, I returned to check to see if I caught anything. And, of course, I didn't.

It's easy for us to take our requests to the Lord. Heck, I like to take my requests to Him and anyone else who wants to pray for me. LOL. The hardest part is the waiting! For me, just sitting and keeping my mouth shut for even five minutes is hard.

However, I know that if I force myself to sit and wait quietly after sharing my list of requests, He will often speak to me. Now, He doesn't speak to me audibly; instead, He gives me thoughts in my mind. He doesn't *always* speak to me right then and there, but forcing myself to sit quietly helps me to remember that my time with God every morning is a TWO-WAY conversation. This spiritual habit WILL change your life if you do it every day!

Wouldn't it be the silliest thing ever to go through the drive-thru, place your order, and never stop and wait to get your food? It's equally important to give God a chance to respond after you've just shared all of your requests with Him, wouldn't you agree?

Today, I challenge you to put this verse into action. I'm right beside you in this challenge. Trust me, I have Attention Deficit Disorder (ADD), so sitting still, quieting my mind, and waiting on the Lord is really hard for me.

I often have to keep a blank notepad close by so when all of those "things" I need to remember to do later flood my thoughts, I can quickly write them down and go right back to focusing on God again. If you're like me, grab a notepad right now.

Start by writing this verse in your journal. Then do what it says: write down your list of requests, and finally take five minutes to sit quietly in His presence. Use a timer if necessary. I did at first. Five minutes is only a suggestion. You can certainly take longer, but that is a good starting point. God knows your heart. Don't get too caught up in the details.

After, write down in your journal anything you felt God speaking to you about. If you didn't hear anything, that is okay. The important thing is that you sat quietly for five minutes.

Remember it takes time to develop a habit, so don't get discouraged if you forget or run out of time or sleep in a couple of mornings. Just keep practicing. Eventually, you will be eager to spend time with God in the morning because you'll know He is always eager to spend time with you!

Today's Prayer:

Lord, I am going to do what You say in Psalm 5:3, Here are my requests (tell Him what you just wrote). I'm now just going to sit in Your presence and wait expectantly. Please help me to focus on You and what You want to say to me. Whether I hear anything or not, starting today, no longer will I rush through my list of requests and run off. I'm going to include a time of silence so that You can speak to me. Now, I'm going to close my mouth and give You my full attention for the next five minutes. In Jesus' name, I pray, AMEN.

PSALM 5:8

Day 5: Wisdom for Direction

"Lead me in the right path, O Lord, or my enemies will conquer me. Make Your way plain for me to follow."
Psalm 5:8 (NLT)

We make hundreds of decisions every day. God wants to be involved in even the smallest of details in your life. The decisions you make this morning can shape how the rest of your day will go, thus potentially influencing the rest of your week and month and on and on.

When David wrote this Psalm, he was being chased by King Saul's army. Maybe you don't have an army of men chasing after you trying to kill you, but you might have an army of negative thoughts that are beating you down at every turn.

Maybe you have a mounting army of distractions keeping you from focusing on what God's called you to do. Maybe you're feeling overpowered by mounting anger, resentment, or bitterness that's threatening to destroy your once happy disposition.

If you are, ask God to lead you in the right path in whatever you're facing in your career, your finances, or your relationships. Ask Him to make His way plain for you to follow. Be specific when you pray. The key here is to be in constant communication with Him every day.

It is much easier to make a correction if you're only one or two steps off the right path. But if you've gone 100 miles down the wrong path, it's going to take a lot longer to get back on track.

Make Psalm 5:8 a part of your daily prayer time. This morning, write it in your journal. Then, write it on a 3x5 index card and keep it with you. You're going to need it for the next step.

Are you ready? Your next step is to memorize this verse. You bought this book for a reason, right? Do you want to get to the end of these 31 days and be the same? Trust me, there is going to be a time when you are facing a decision, and there's no time to go hunting for that 3x5 index card.

Today's Prayer:

Lord, lead me in the right path, or my enemies will conquer me. Some of the enemies I'm facing right now are (fill in the blank). Please make Your way plain for me to follow. I also pray that You will help me memorize this verse so the next time I need to make a decision, this verse will fill my mind, reminding me to always look to You first for guidance. In Jesus' name, I pray, AMEN.

PSALM 5:12

Day 6:
Wisdom for Growing a Strong Faith

"Surely, Lord You bless the righteous; You surround them with Your favor as with a shield."
Psalm 5:12 (NIV)

If you're like me; you don't feel very righteous most of the time. The problem, however, is really how we perceive the meaning of this word. Let me open your eyes to perhaps another way to see this word and its meaning. Romans 3:23-26 (NLT) says:

> *"For everyone has sinned; we all fall short of God's glorious standard. Yet God freely and graciously declares that we are righteous. He did this through Christ Jesus when He freed us from the penalty for our sins. For God presented Jesus as the sacrifice for sin. People are made right with God when they believe that Jesus sacrificed his life, shedding his blood. This sacrifice shows that God was being fair when He held back and did not punish those who sinned in times past, for He*

was looking ahead and including them in what He would do in this present time. God did this to demonstrate His righteousness, for He himself is fair and just, and He declares sinners to be right in His sight when they believe in Jesus."

Do we not have the coolest heavenly Father ever?

The blessings promised in Psalm 5 aren't *only* for those super spiritually strong people. We are declared righteous when we believe in Jesus. You and I are included, warts and all!

I know what some of you might be thinking, "Well, I'm declared righteous. That's great. But I haven't been feeling shielded with His favor lately." I'm going to go out on a limb here and say that just maybe, deep down the real struggle is your lack of belief. I often struggle with this issue too.

Romans 10:17 tells us that faith comes by hearing, and hearing by the word of Christ. So the antidote to our lack of belief is to be reading God's word, DAILY. The more you spend time reading God's word, the more you will realize how much He loves you, and your belief (faith) in Him will begin to grow stronger and stronger.

Today's Prayer:

Lord, You promise in Psalm 5:12 that You bless the righteous and surround them with Your favor as with a shield. I ask for Your blessing and for You to surround me with Your favor today. I ask for You to show me blessings that I have overlooked. I want to deepen my faith, so give me a hunger for reading Your word so my faith will grow stronger. In Jesus' name, I pray, AMEN.

PSALM 9:1

Day 7:
Wisdom for When I Need a Thankful Heart

"I will give thanks to You, Lord, with all my heart; I will tell of all Your wonderful deeds".
Psalm 9:1 (NIV)

Many times, I am so eager to tell God what I really need and what I really want that I forget to praise Him for everything He has already done. But I have found that when I force myself to start my prayer time each morning with what I'm thankful for, it transforms my heart much faster than when I jump to my list of requests first.

I encourage you to do the same. I know it seems strange to start with what you're thankful for first, especially when you're totally overwhelmed with doubt, fear, or a really frustrating circumstance. Trust me, this works.

Starting today, begin your prayer time with God by thinking back over the past week or month and write in your journal two or three things for which you are thankful.

Sometimes, if I'm having a particularly rough morning, I will start with thanking Him for something I've already thanked Him for in the past. Like this morning; I thanked Him for blessing me with the opportunity to have more time to write even though I thanked Him for this same thing just yesterday.

Here's today's challenge for you. Choose one of the things you wrote in your journal and share it with someone. Not in a "show-off" kind of way, but the next time you get ready to tell your friend something bad that just happened, instead choose to share something for which you're grateful. You will be doing what the second part of what Psalm 9:1 says to do... *"I will tell of all your wonderful deeds."*

I promise that if you make it a habit every day to start your prayer time with something you're thankful for; you will feel your heart begin to fill with joy and gratitude. And, before you know it, your faith will increase because you will realize just how much He really has done for you!

Today's Prayer:

Lord, I will give thanks to You, with all my heart. I thank You for (fill in the blank). And, if I start to doubt You're hearing me, remind me of everything You've already done for me. I also pray that You will remind me to share these wonderful things You've done for me with others. In Jesus' name, I pray, AMEN.

PSALM 9:2

Day 8:
Wisdom for Defeating Worry

"I will be filled with joy because of You. I will sing praises to Your name, O Most High."
Psalm 9:2 (NLT)

Need a shot of joy in your day? Here's how to get it, but it's not what you think!

If you're feeling weighed down with worry or drowning in overwhelming stress this morning, put Psalm 9:2 into action by singing a couple of praise songs before starting your prayer time with God today. Watch and see how much closer you will feel to Him when you start your prayer time this way.

Singing praise and worship songs is a regular part of my prayer time with God every morning. With my A.D.D. I tend to have a hard time quieting and calming my mind and heart. Singing a worship song quickly gets my mind focused on God and tuned in to

Him. If it helps you to tune out other background noise, use earphones. If you're home alone, crank it up! That's what I do. ☺

If you're going through a really tough time in your life, playing worship songs helps lift your mood. If you don't know any good worship songs or can't think of any with lyrics that are directed to God, here are a few that I use:

- "Word of God Speak" by MercyMe
- "Revelation Song" by Phillips, Craig & Dean
- "Great are You Lord" by All Sons and Daughters

Pick songs that you can sing along with and that have lyrics that are like a prayer to God. The songs I listed above are good examples. If you go to my YouTube channel, I update my worship song playlist with good songs all the time. You can find a link to my YouTube channel by going to my website: www.straighttalkforwomen.com.

Be careful not to do what I did just this morning. I was getting ready to have my prayer time and wanted to download a new song I had just heard at church. I went to look for it online and before I knew it, I had wasted like 45 minutes. I got sidetracked listening to some other songs I found. Luckily, I had more time today, so I didn't waste my entire prayer time looking for that song. By the way, I still haven't found the specific song I was originally looking for! Yep, that's how easily I get distracted.

Here is the challenge for you today. Go find a couple of good worship songs that you really like and buy them. This way, you will have them ready for tomorrow's prayer time and for whenever you feel down and need a boost.

Don't just listen to them...SING along! If you can't sing very well, turn up the music louder than your voice so you don't have to hear yourself. That's what I do. Before you know it, you will feel the joy filling your heart as you sing to God. I don't know how He does it, but He does.

Today's Prayer:

Lord, because of You, I will be filled with joy today. I will sing praises to You Lord. Please help me to find some special worship songs to use every morning that will help me tune in to hearing Your voice and that will fill my heart with joy. And when I'm feeling down and start to worry, help me to choose to worship instead. In Jesus' name, I pray, AMEN.

PSALM 9:10

Day 9: Wisdom for Building Trust

"Those who know Your name, trust in You. For You, O Lord, do not abandon those who search for You."
Psalm 9:10 (NLT)

A couple of years ago, we went with our good friends and their two daughters to Jamaica for our summer vacation. The whole week basically consisted of floating around in the pool, lying out on the beach, and eating. Besides gaining 5 pounds; I felt like I got to know them so much more than the almost 18 years we've spent living next door to them.

The same is true in our relationship with God. The more time we spend with Him on a daily basis the more we will really get to know Him. As a result, our trust in Him will grow.

He is telling us plainly in Psalm 9:10 that we won't trust someone we don't know. Just because I happen to live next door to someone doesn't mean I trust him or her. I bet you have neighbors who live on your street that you don't know or can't remember their names. They probably wouldn't be the first on your list of people to call to watch your kids for a weekend. Likewise, we might keep a Bible on our nightstand or say a prayer as we run out the door to work in the morning but still not really trust that God knows and cares about what we're going through.

There's just no substitute for spending time with God regularly. Do you want to feel more secure and worry less when these 31 days are over? The answer is simple: get to know the One who loves you more than anyone else, the One who knows everything about you - the good, the bad, and the ugly - yet will never abandon you.

Today's Prayer:

Lord, You say in Psalm 9:10 that You know those who know Your name and trust in You and that You do not abandon those who search for You. I want to trust in You more. Give me a renewed desire to spend time with You every day. Give me a hunger to spend time reading Your word. Show me the areas where I'm not trusting in You. Show me things I need to cut from my schedule so that I can have more time with You. In Jesus' name, I pray, AMEN.

PSALM 16:8

Day 10: Wisdom for When I Lose My Focus

"I keep my eyes always on the Lord. With Him at my right hand, I will not be shaken."
Psalm 16:8 (NIV)

Do you worry? Let me ask that question a different way. Do others say you worry a lot? Do you hear statements like, "Don't worry about it," or "You worry too much," or "Don't worry, everything will work out?" I've been hearing these statements a lot lately.

I guess maybe I'm forgetting to keep my eyes on the Lord, so I'm worrying more. How about you? Any of those statements above sound familiar?

Maybe, for you; it's a daily struggle not to worry about how you're going to pay a bill that's due next week, your marriage situation, or what's going on with your kids.

The importance of keeping our focus on Jesus instead of worrying about our problems reminds me of that famous story in the New Testament about Peter getting out of the boat to go see Jesus who is walking on the water. All excited, Peter jumps out and starts walking toward Jesus. When he takes his eyes off Jesus and looks down at the waves below; he immediately sinks. This is a perfect example of what can happen when we take our eyes off Jesus and start focusing on our problems. We will begin to sink just like Peter did. But, if we do what Psalm 16:8 tells us to do and keep our eyes on the Lord, we won't be shaken because the whole time He is right beside us.

He is right beside you right now. Whether you're sitting at your desk at work, sitting on the couch at home, sitting at the kitchen table, or sitting in the doctor's office waiting room. He is saying to you right now, "Keep your eyes on me and not your problem. I'm right beside you, so you will not be shaken."

Today's Prayer:

Lord, help me keep my eyes on You and not my problems today. When I start to focus on (fill in the blank) instead of You, remind me that with You at my right hand, I will not be shaken. Lord, You know what I will be facing today so help me to feel Your presence throughout the day. Give me confidence to handle (fill in the blank) knowing You are right beside me always. In Jesus' name, I pray, AMEN.

PSALM 19:7

Day 11:
Wisdom for Becoming Wise

"The instructions of the Lord are perfect, reviving the soul. The decrees of the Lord are trustworthy, making wise the simple."
Psalm 19:7 (NLT)

God tells us plainly in Psalm 19:7 how to be revived and become wise. If your faith feels stale or stagnated, read His *perfect* and *trustworthy instructions,* A.K.A. the Bible. Your soul will be revived, and you will become wise. That's right; there is no special formula.

The problem isn't that we didn't know this truth already; it's that we don't do it. We ask our friends for advice. We read that latest self-help book to find insight. We search the Internet for answers. Once we've exhausted everything and everyone else first; then we go to the Bible.

Don't get me wrong. Our friends, self-help books, and the Internet are all very helpful; however, they shouldn't replace, or come before seeking God and His word for encouragement and wisdom. His word is 100% perfect and 100% trustworthy; but our friends, self-help books, and the Internet...not so much. Would you agree?

If you desire for God to revive your faith and fill you with wisdom, read His word. If reading the Bible is a struggle for you, here are a few suggestions:

1. Choose an easy translation. I suggest the New Living Translation (NLT) or the New International Version (NIV). These two are my personal favorites.

2. Read for depth not distance. Don't try to read as fast as you can to see how far you can get in one sitting. It's like taking a cross country trip. You'll learn a lot more about each state if you drive than if you fly. Choose a chapter or even just a paragraph or two, depending how much time you have.

3. Start with the New Testament. The first four books; Matthew, Mark, Luke, and John each explain the life and events of Jesus and His ministry through their own individual perspectives. I didn't get this until I had read the entire Bible through four times. I'm a little slow.☺

I challenge you to start today. Sit for ten minutes and dig deep into God's word. It will revive your soul and fill you with wisdom beyond what you could ever imagine. This is an essential first step to becoming wise.

Today's Prayer:

Lord, Psalm 19:7 tells me that Your word is perfect and trustworthy. It will revive me and make me wise. Please help me make reading Your word a priority. Open my eyes to see where my priorities are not aligned with Your will. I pray that when I start reading in a few minutes You will block all distractions that would keep me from hearing You. In Jesus' name, I pray, AMEN.

PSALM 19:14

Day 12:
Wisdom for Gaining Control of My Mouth

"May the words of my mouth and the meditation of my heart be pleasing to You O' Lord, my rock, my redeemer."
Psalm 19:14 (NLT)

Want to reduce frustration significantly in your relationships? Make this verse your morning prayer to God every day. Better yet, memorize it. There are plenty of things out of our control in life. The mouth, however, isn't one of them.

If we would just take five seconds to think before we start running off our mouths, we really could save ourselves a lot of unnecessary grief.

We cannot control what others say to us or about us, but we can control how we respond. I'm going to challenge you to become a better ***T.H.I.N.K.E.R.*** I took a well-known acrostic and *kicked it up a notch.* LOL.

Be a better T.H.I.N.K.E.R. - 7 questions to ask yourself before opening your mouth:

Truthful - Is what I'm about to say, truthful, and not an exaggeration or a half truth?

Helpful - Is what I'm about to say helpful? I might want to say it, but is it really going to help this situation?

Inspiring - Is what I'm about to say, inspiring? Will it have a positive impact?

Necessary - Is what I'm about to say necessary? Right now? In this situation? With all who are present?

Kind - Is what I'm about to say kind? Or can I say it in a kind way?

Encouraging- Is what I'm about to say encouraging? Will my words build them up?

Respectful - Is what I'm about to say respectful? Or can I say it in a respectful manner?

If the answer is "no" to any of the questions, then you should hold off on what you want to say until you've had more time to pray about it.

Not only do we want our words to be pleasing but also the meditation of our hearts. The motive behind what you want to say comes from your heart. Ask God to examine not only your words but also the motive behind them.

It's my guess that the number of arguments we get into could be cut in half if we work on gaining control of our mouths.

Today's Prayer:

Lord, may the words of my mouth and the meditation of my heart be pleasing to You O' Lord, my rock, my redeemer. I pray You will help me become a better thinker! Examine my own heart's motives and show me anything that is unpleasing to You. Keep me from hurting anyone with my words. In Jesus' name, I pray, AMEN.

PSALMS 25:4-5

Day 13:
Wisdom for Choosing the Right Path

"Show me the right path, O lord; point out the road for me to follow. Lead me by Your truth and teach me, for You are the God who saves me. All day long I put my hope in You."
Psalms 25:4-5 (NLT)

Feeling confused? Not sure which path to take? This verse is a good one to pray. When you ask for God's direction, just be sure to listen. Then, let Him lead you by His truth. In verse five where it says, "Lead me by your truth," David is referring to God's word. Guidance is often found directly through reading His word. So, if you feel God is telling you to do something; but it contradicts with what it says in His word; you should question what you're hearing.

If you're still unclear, keep praying and reading His word. Continue to seek His guidance. You might also ask a close friend to pray for you as well. What you don't want to do is get too eager and run ahead of God. I have done this so many times. Every time I run too fast and get ahead of God, I fall flat on my face. But He graciously gives me another chance to get it right. And He'll even give me a third and fourth chance if necessary.

I once attended a sales training workshop, and the instructor taught us to "Go Slow to Go Fast." In sales, this concept means that it's sometimes better to slow down and spend more time gathering information about what your potential customer needs before jumping right to all the cool gadgets you have to offer. If you spend more time in the beginning asking the right questions, you'll be able to identify more quickly the exact product or service that will best help your customer.

We should implement this "Go Slow to Go Fast" idea when we are in need of guidance in our personal life. If we slow down, take more time to pray, read God's word, and seek His will, more likely, we will make better decisions.

Today's Prayer:

Lord, I pray Psalms 25:4-5: Show me the right path, point out the road for me to follow. Lead me by Your truth and teach me, for You are the God who saves me. All day long, I put my hope in You. I'm feeling unsure about (fill in the blank). Please lead me to the right scripture that will give me wisdom in making this decision. Keep me from getting ahead of You and messing things up. Help me to gain the knowledge needed to make good choices. If there is any sin in my life that would keep me from hearing Your voice clearly, point it out to me so that I can repent and get back on track. In Jesus' name, I pray, AMEN.

PSALM 25:8

Day 14: Wisdom for When I Want to Give Up on Someone

"The Lord is good and does what is right; He shows the proper path to those who go astray."
Psalm 25:8 (NLT)

Do you know someone who has gone astray? I do. My heart breaks as I watch them drift down that dark path. Sometimes, my thoughts get the best of me, and I start to feel that hopeless feeling in the pit of my stomach that whispers, *They'll never return. It's too late for them. They've gone too far away from God. Just give up. Why keep praying?* But in the back of my mind, I know that God is totally capable of bringing them back. I've seen this happen several times in my own life.

At church camp one summer, there was a girl in our cabin who wasn't a Christian. She just came because her friend begged her to go. The rest of us were mostly new, "baby" believers. With all of our new zeal for God and eagerness to save all of our lost friends, we all began an intense mission to pray for her to be saved that very week during camp. None of us had "*matured*" enough to think we couldn't make it happen in four days.

Night after night as the speaker preached his powerful message, we all looked at each other, smiled or giggled as all teen girls do for no apparent reason, and began to pray. Each night, he asked us to bow our heads and close our eyes as he presented the altar call to anyone wanting to ask Jesus into his or her heart to come to the front. Many of us occasionally peeked over to see if there was any movement, but the girl we were praying for remained quiet in her seat.

The fifth night, as the preacher gave his last altar call, we all held hands and prayed earnestly for God to move. Suddenly, our friend leaped out of her chair as if she was being ejected out of the cockpit of a fighter jet in a death spin. As she lunged toward the aisle, her foot caught the chair she was sitting in practically dragging it with her. Because the chair made such a commotion, almost everyone looked over to see what happened. Instantly, our hearts exploded with joy and excitement. We were all high-fiving like we had just won the world series!

Of course, we didn't save her; God did. But what we did do was BELIEVE He would save her so we never, for one second, even considered not praying. It's like we knew it was just a matter of time. She had no chance against our powerful prayers to our really cool God who could do anything.

Now that I'm much older, why is it that I often doubt my really cool God whom I once believed could do anything? This is precisely why we must be relentless in our commitment to read His word daily. Psalm 25:8 reminds us of our amazing God who will show the proper path to those who go astray. We just need to stand on this promise and NEVER STOP PRAYING!

Will you join me? I dare you! Start praying today for that person whom you're thinking about right now, the one who has gone astray, AND REFUSE TO STOP UNTIL YOU SEE GOD'S MIRACLE!

Today's Prayer:

Lord, You are so good, and You always do what is right. You promise to show the proper path to those who go astray, so I ask You to please show (person's name) the proper path for his/her life. Lord, I will never stop praying for (person's name). I pray that any time I start to doubt You, remind me of Psalm 25:8. And when I don't understand what You're doing, help me to just keep trusting and keep praying! In Jesus' name, I pray, AMEN.

PSALM 25:9

Day 15:
Wisdom for Learning to be Humble

"He leads the humble in doing right, teaching them His way."

Psalm 25:9 (NLT)

I don't know about you, but I want nothing more than to be led by God to do what is right and be taught His way. I looked up the word "humble" just to be sure I understood what it meant. Here's the Webster's Dictionary definition; *Having or showing a consciousness of one's shortcomings; modest.*

So, Psalm 25:9 means that if I am *consciously aware of and willing to admit my shortcomings*; He will lead me in doing right and teach me His way. Sounds easy enough, right? We just need to be honest about our hang-ups, and He will lead us in doing what is right and teach us His ways. Hmmm, let's think about this verse a little more.

During my prayer time that morning, I asked God, "So what does it look like to live this verse out each day?" I'm going to get real with you right now. Here's what God brought to my attention:

1. Don't making excuses for my lack of follow through on something such as admitting when I drop the ball and apologize.

2. Don't attempt to "puff up" myself when opportunities present themselves. Remember, *"I'm no better a person than the next."*

3. Choose to have a "serving" attitude when I have to do something I feel is beneath me or not in my job description.

So, how's that for transparency. Did you relate to any of the things God brought to my attention? I totally thought I had that "humble" thing down, but after talking to God about it, boy, was I wrong.

Philippians 2:13 (NLT) is another verse that I will be clinging to as I work on becoming more humble, maybe it will help you: *"For God is working in you, giving you the desire and the power to do what pleases Him."* As you pray this morning, write down anything that comes to your mind in your journal.

Today's Prayer:

Lord, I want You to lead me in doing what is right, and I also want You to teach me Your ways. Psalm 25:9 tells me that You will do this for those who are humble. I ask You to show me areas where I need to be more humble. Make them very clear to me today. I pray You will give me the wisdom to be humble when tempted to cover up my shortcomings or when tempted to be boastful or arrogant. In Jesus' name, I pray, AMEN.

PSALMS 25:12-13

Day 16:
Wisdom for Living a Prosperous Life

"Who are those who fear the LORD? He will show them the path they should choose. They will live in prosperity, and their children will inherit the land."
Psalms 25:12-13 (NLT)

Did you know that with every decision you make, you're paving a way for your future and your family's future? Yep. The choices you make today choose tomorrow's path. Are you making the right ones? Are you sure? Your future and your family's future depend on it. Do you want to be confident in the path you're choosing? If you do; I have good news. The promise in Psalm 25:12 tells us how we can be confident in the path we choose, and in verse 13 we learn the benefits.

So how do we become confident in the choices we make, since they dictate the paths we will be on tomorrow? We do it by becoming a woman who *"fears the Lord."* I know what you're going to ask next. *What in the heck is that supposed to mean?* I'm glad you asked. I wanted to know, too, so I looked up the definition of the word "fear."

Like you, I knew there was another definition besides the *"home alone and you hear a noise upstairs"* kind of fear. Here's the definition from the Webster's Dictionary:

Fear: noun - #2 "awe, reverence" *verb* – "to be in awe of"

Now, you need a good picture of the kind of awe/reverence we're talking about. It's the kind that you would have for the One who created the stars, the moon, the earth, and the sun. It's the kind you would have for the One who created everything in our universe in order to create YOU and me.

Yep, that's right. The very air we're breathing is possible because God made everything in our universe work together specifically allow us to the ability to live and breathe and walk on this earth. Why did God do this? Because the Bible tells us that God is love, and He wanted a family to love. Knowing that true love is real *only* when it's freely given and received, He created us with the freedom to choose whether or not we would love Him back.

Now, if that isn't deserving of our utmost awe and reverence, I don't know what is. And that is just the beginning of how awesome our God is. I don't have the time to go into the rest; that is a whole other book.

So how do we show reverence for the God who created the entire universe for us?

Here are three steps:

1. Acknowledge and willingly accept Him as your Lord and Savior.

2. Seek to get to know Him more and more each day by talking to Him (prayer) and reading the book He wrote specifically for you, the Bible.

3. Do what He tells you to do, immediately and without hesitation or reservation.

Psalms 25:12-13 tells us we will have three benefits if we become women who fear God.

Here are three benefits:

1. He will show us the path we should choose.

2. He will give us prosperity enabling us to succeed and thrive in this life.

3. Our children will reap the benefits as well.

So my question to you is what are you going to do now? Keep doing the same thing you've been doing? How's that working for you? If you do what I have suggested, you will grow in reverence and awe of God, your creator.

How do I know? Because it's been happening in my life over the past 30 plus years. The more I seek to know Him the more I am in true amazement at the awesome depth of His love for me. Even though I continue to make mistakes, He loves me the same and somehow miraculously uses my most embarrassing failures to bring hope and encouragement to others. He can do the same for you!

Today's Prayer:

Lord, first I want to thank You for creating me and loving me in spite of all my mistakes. I pray that You will make me into a woman who fears You. Give me an unquenchable thirst to know You more each day. Do not let me become complacent in my faith but fill me with a desire to grow. I know that my choices today shape my direction tomorrow, so I ask that You show me the right path to choose. In Jesus' name, I pray, AMEN.

PSALM 25:15

Day 17: Wisdom for Escaping the Traps of My Enemies

"My eyes are always on the Lord, for He rescues me from the traps of my enemies."
Psalm 25:15 (NLT)

What's got you trapped? When David wrote about enemies; he was facing real enemies who were physically chasing him in order to kill him. Because of where we live, most of us today don't face the threat of real enemies like in David's time or in other countries. Therefore, when we read verses like this one in Psalms that mentions "enemies," sometimes we might not see how they apply to us. I would challenge you to think again.

The enemy is alive and well among us. He seeks to steal our happiness, kill our hope, and destroy our relationships. The traps he uses are well disguised, such as the trap that implies that busyness equals significance.

Another trap might be the lure of pursuing comfort and convenience no matter what the cost or number of credit card payments. How about the lure of prestige that a fancy title at work will provide? Any of these traps hit home for you? Maybe your trap is the pursuit of accomplishment at the sacrifice of relationship.

Maybe the trap that lures you is believing that good parents provide for their kids well into their adult years in spite of mounting debt. Another trap that's disguised really well for us moms is the lure that being a "super mom" will produce super kids. I've discovered that a super mom usually produces super spoiled kids and a shallow, weak marriage. I tell wives all the time, "The best way to love your kids is to love their dad!"

So what's got you trapped? Whatever it is; you're not alone. All of the traps I just mentioned are all the ones off my personal list. The good news is that God can rescue us from them. Just keep your eyes on Him.

Here are four steps to help you get out and stay out of Satan's traps:

1. Ask God to reveal to you anything that is a potential trap in your life. (good verse to memorize – Psalms 139:23-24)

2. Keep your eyes on God every day by talking to Him in prayer and reading His word. (memorize today's verse: Psalm 25:15)

3. If you're in a trap right now, stop trying to rescue yourself and just admit it to God. Here's a little secret... He already

knows you're trapped. He won't be surprised. Your repentant heart is what He desires to rescue.

4. Share what has you trapped or tends to lure you with one other person for support and accountability.

I'll ask you again, "What's got you trapped?" Ask God today to rescue you. He's waiting for you to ask.

Today's Prayer:

Lord, Psalm 25:15 reminds me that You are the one who rescues me from the traps of my enemies. I admit to You today that I have been trapped by (fill in the blank), and I need You to rescue me. I will no longer try to rescue myself. I will keep my eyes focused on You, Lord. When something threatens to trap me again, bring to my mind Psalm 25:15, so that I won't be lured in again. In Jesus' name, I pray, AMEN.

PSALMS 27:7-8

Day 18:
Wisdom for Eliminating Distractions

"Hear me as I pray, O' Lord. Be merciful and answer me!
My heart has heard You say, 'Come and talk with me.' And
my heart responds, 'Lord, I am coming.' "
Psalms 27:7-8 (NLT)

Do you notice who's doing the calling, and who's doing the responding here? God is the one pursuing a conversation with us. Think about this important detail for just a minute. If your husband, boyfriend, or adult child said to you "Come, let's hang out and talk," would you be excited? I know I would.

But how often do we ignore the calling of our heavenly father to come and talk with Him? Or, are we bombarded with so many distractions; we never end up actually talking to Him at all? God, the creator of this entire universe, calls to me to talk with Him, and I'm too busy checking my email...Really? But, as soon as you-know-what hits the fan, I'm crying out to Him for help.

Sound familiar? If so, we have something in common because this is the struggle I have many mornings. I'm eager to say, "Lord, I am coming," but when I sit down in front of my computer, it's like my email program reaches out and grabs hold of my head, forcing me to see the unread messages that seem to be —pulsating as they sit in my inbox. Or if it isn't my email pawing at me, my adorable little miniature Schnauzer is trying to get into my lap.

Another distraction that gets me every time is TIME! The clock seems to speed up when I open my Bible in the morning. The more I look at it, the more I see the minutes slipping away faster and faster. Never mind that I got up late, leaving only 15 minutes to meet with the "One" I claim to be the most important person in my life!

The other thing that constantly distracts me are the millions of tasks that start circling in my head just as I start to listen to my favorite worship song. Then, there's my cell phone vibrating every couple minutes alerting me of a new text message *–ugh!*

Do any of these distractions threaten your morning prayer time? If so, here are three things I do every morning. Maybe they will help you, too.

>1. Refuse to look at your email inbox until your prayer time with God is finished. *BTW* – I failed and wasted ten minutes on this one just this morning. I'm a work in progress.

>2. Keep a blank sheet of paper or sticky notes nearby to jot down those pesky things-to-do thoughts that flood your mind as you begin to pray.

3. Put your phone on airplane mode so that you don't get distracted by the incoming notifications.

Today's Prayer:

Lord, I know You want to spend time with me every morning. Help me to make this time with You a priority. Help me to go to bed earlier so I can spend more time with You in the morning. Help me eliminate these specific distractions: (list everything that distracts you during your morning prayer time). In Jesus' name, I pray, AMEN.

PSALMS 27:11-13

Day 19:
Wisdom for Handling Criticism

"Teach me how to live, O Lord. Lead me along the right path, for my enemies are waiting for me. Do not let me fall into their hands. For they accuse me of things I've never done; with every breath they threaten me with violence. Yet I am confident I will see the Lord's goodness while I am here in the land of the living."
Psalms 27:11-13 (NLT)

Have you ever been falsely accused of something? Have your motives ever been maligned or questioned? Have your words ever been turned around and maliciously used against you? If you have, I'm glad you're reading this devotional because these verses are for you. You can pray them to God today.

I have prayed these verses in the past when I've personally experienced some heavy criticism for my beliefs and values. I have even recited these verses out loud during my prayer time in the past. After reading through the Old Testament and learning how David went through several years of being hunted by King Saul's army; I trust he knew what it was like to be falsely accused and despised.

I hate to break the news to you, but if you start doing what I've suggested in this 31-day devotional; expect to be criticized. As you begin pursuing godly wisdom, there will be people who will challenge and criticize you.

If you're being unjustly criticized for your beliefs or moral standards, know that God sees exactly what you're going through. Like David, you too can be confident that you will see the Lord's goodness while in the land of the living.

If you're taking a stand for what is right, God will protect you. However, how He does it isn't always the same. Sometimes, God removes us from the situation or sometimes He removes the enemies. Other times, God chooses not to remove us or the enemies but instead makes us strong enough to endure.

Today's Prayer:

Lord, teach me how to live. Lead me along the right path, for my enemies are waiting for me. Do not let me fall into their hands, for they accuse me of things I've never done. With every breath, they threaten me with violence, yet I am confident I will see the Lord's goodness while I am here in the land of the living. If You choose not to remove the enemies from my life, give me the strength and confidence to endure and ignore their criticism. In Jesus' name, I pray, AMEN.

PSALM 27:14

Day 20: Wisdom for What to Do When I Must Wait

"Wait patiently for the Lord. Be brave and courageous. Yes, wait patiently for the Lord."
Psalm 27:14 (NLT)

As I read this verse during my prayer time with God; it seemed to leap off the page and grab me by the cheeks as if to say, "Do you get it? You've read this verse a million times, but do you really get it?" At first thought, it seems like an oxymoron, right? How can I wait patiently AND be brave and courageous at the same time? I view the word "patient" as a passive word, and the words "brave and courageous" as active words. Wouldn't you agree?

Of course, out of curiosity, I decided to look up the word patient in the dictionary. What I discovered is that nowhere does it say "to sit and do nothing." In fact, it provides three definitions: 1. Enduring pain, trouble, and so forth without complaining; 2. Calmly tolerating delay, confusion, and so forth, and 3. Diligently persevering.

There are two amazing insights I want you to get in this verse:

1. Waiting patiently on the Lord doesn't mean to sit and do nothing. We are to be brave and courageous. When I was in a situation once where I was forced to wait on God, I sat and sulked the whole time but God wanted me to grow stronger and gain courage during my time of waiting.

He wants you to do the same. Whether you're waiting for your husband to come to the Lord; waiting for a job opportunity; or waiting for your health to improve, do what you can to become stronger emotionally, mentally, spiritually, and physically.

You can grow spiritually by spending more time with God and reading His word. You can grow stronger mentally by learning all you can while you're waiting. You can grow stronger emotionally by getting counseling or joining a support group. You can grow stronger physically by joining a gym or establishing better eating habits.

2. Waiting patiently is calmly and diligently persevering without complaining. During my times of waiting, I was definitely not calm or persevering without complaining. Instead, I spent a lot of time whining about what I couldn't do.

Wherever God has you is where He wants you, or you wouldn't be there. Go back and read that sentence again. Get the point? As much as you or I may dislike where we are right now, God has us there for a purpose. Maybe it's to teach you to trust Him, or maybe it's to get your attention. Maybe it's to grow you up or to strengthen or prepare you for what is ahead. We may not understand or like it, but He's God, and we're not.

Today's Prayer:

Lord, help me to learn to be bold, courageous and patient while I wait on You right now for (fill in the blank). Please forgive me for sitting and sulking and even complaining. I know there is a reason I am where I am. Please help me to see what I can do while I'm waiting. Show me areas where I need to grow stronger during this time of waiting. Even though I don't understand fully why I'm still waiting, I am thankful for (fill in the blank) right now. From now on, when I start to complain help me to think of one thing I can choose to be thankful for. In Jesus' name, I pray, AMEN.

PSALMS 28:6-7

Day 21:
Wisdom for When I'm Paralyzed by Indecision

"Praise the Lord! For He has heard my cry for mercy. The Lord is my strength and shield. I trust Him with all my heart. He helps me, and my heart is filled with joy. I burst out in songs of thanksgiving."
Psalms 28:6-7 (NLT)

Have you ever felt paralyzed by indecisiveness? I have. I've really struggled with this issue many times in my life. I become so afraid of failing that I over analyze my decisions to the point that I am frozen and can't go in any direction. I've made some really big mistakes in the past, so the fear of making mistakes has become quite a stumbling block for me.

I am constantly double checking and triple checking to see if my decision is the best one possible. With one recent writing project I was working on, I became overwhelmed and consumed by the tiniest of details to the point where I had come to a complete stop and couldn't seem to make any forward progress. I would make one decision, fearfully second guess my decision, and change it back. I felt paralyzed.

Finally, I literally cried out to God for mercy for getting so afraid of such minor details. As I prayed, I felt my heart fill with joy and a sense of relief came over me. I knew He had heard my cry for help. I felt so relieved that I could trust in His promise in Psalm 28 that He truly is my strength and shield. You can experience this same joy!

Are you fearful of making mistakes? Do you often feel paralyzed by indecision? If you struggle with indecisiveness like me, or anything else, cry out to God for mercy. Just admit whatever it is that has you stuck in fear. God wants to help you. You don't have to "figure it out" on your own.

When you call on Him for mercy, He will help you. Don't go another day living in fear of making mistakes. He is your strength and shield. As soon as you cry out to Him, He will help you. Then sit back and watch as your heart begins to fill with joy.

Today's Prayer:

Lord, I cry out to You for mercy. I am overwhelmed with making a mistake with (fill in the blank). I feel paralyzed with fear and ask for Your mercy right now. I trust You with all my heart and know You will help me. Whenever I start to become consumed by this fear again, remind me that You are my strength and shield and You will help me. In Jesus' name, I pray, AMEN.

PSALMS 29:4-5

Day 22:
Wisdom for Understanding God's Power

"The voice of the Lord is powerful; the voice of the Lord is majestic. The voice of the Lord splits the mighty cedars; the lord shatters the cedars of Lebanon."
Psalms 29:4-5 (NLT)

It's really hard for me to picture in my mind the sheer power that it would take to split mighty cedars with your voice. Heck, I can barely blow out birthday candles. I can't imagine having that kind of power. However, several years ago, my daughter made a strange yet amazingly perceptive observation of this sometimes hard-to-wrap-our-heads-around concept.

One evening, she and I were driving home when she looked out the window and saw that there was a full moon. She said, "You know, the moon is kind of like the pupil of God's eye." Her description, perhaps, is the perfect word picture to help us visualize just how big and powerful our God truly is. This mental picture is precisely what we need to remember when we're feeling overwhelmed by our circumstances.

Not only is our heavenly Father magnificently great and all powerful, He is also very much interested in the small, seemingly insignificant details of our lives. Jesus explains just how much He cares in Matthew 10:29-31(NLT): *"What is the price of two sparrows—one copper coin? But not a single sparrow can fall to the ground without your Father knowing it. And the very hairs on your head are all numbered. So don't be afraid; you are more valuable to God than a whole flock of sparrows."*

I encourage you today to remember three things when you come upon an overwhelming challenge:

1. We can know that because God's voice is powerful, memorizing what He has said in the Bible is a powerful tool we can use for defeating negative and fearful thoughts.

2. If God's voice is powerful enough to split mighty cedar trees, He is certainly big enough to get us through whatever we're facing.

3. Our God, though big and mighty, loves us so much that He knows even how many hairs are on our head and every time they've been colored, curled, straightened, or permed. You are loved by a magnificently powerful God who is ready to go with you today wherever you have to go and who wants to help you do whatever it is that you have to do.

God's word is powerful! If you haven't yet memorized any verses, I challenge you to start today by memorizing Psalms 29:4-5. Then, work on these next: Philippians 2:13, Proverbs 3:5-7, Philippians 4:6-7, and Psalms 139:23-24. These are essential verses to memorize when you are pursuing godly wisdom.

Today's Prayer:

Lord, help me to remember just how big and powerful You truly are. Thank You for loving me and being interested in even the tiny little details of my life. Help me to pick some good verses to memorize so that when negative or fearful thoughts come into my head, I can defeat them with the power of Your word. In Jesus' name, I pray, AMEN.

PSALM 29:11

Day 23:
Wisdom for When I'm Out of DIY Strength

"The Lord gives His people strength. The Lord blesses them with peace."
Psalm 29:11 (NLT)

The whole "Do-It-Yourself" phrase has exploded with the launch of Pinterest. We don't even say "Do-It-Yourself" anymore. We say "DIY" There are so many amazingly clever DIY ideas you can find on Pinterest. Then we can't leave out YouTube. That's another go-to site for when you need to know how to do something and don't want to hire an expert. Anytime I need to know how to do something; I immediately Google it and look for the YouTube videos.

We even used a YouTube video when the icemaker broke in our refrigerator. It is crazy how you can get step-by-step instructions on what parts to order and how to replace each one of them from a YouTube video. We probably saved at least $150 fixing the icemaker ourselves instead of calling out a service repair tech from the manufacturer.

No doubt, social media sites are great for finding DIY solutions for fixing things around the house.

However, your life is NOT A **DIY** PROJECT! We must remember from where our strength for life comes. Psalm 29:11 tells us it comes from our loving heavenly Father. He alone gives the kind of strength and peace we need to get through what we're going through.

Have you been trying get through life as if it were a DIY project? So, how's that working for you? Romans 12:2 (NLT) tells us, *"Don't copy the behavior and customs of this world, but let God transform you into a new person by changing the way you think."* Maybe you've been raised to believe that if you want to get ahead, you have to do-it-yourself. Don't expect any hand-outs in life, right? Well, I challenge you to give up on that belief.

You don't have enough strength to get through this life successfully on your own. When you start to feel tired, depressed, lonely, irritated, hopeless, discouraged, or apathetic, it means you've used up all the DIY strength you had, and it is time to plug into God; the source of our strength and peace.

How do you plug in? Picture yourself as a cell phone and Jesus as the cell phone charger. Now picture your Bible as a giant electrical outlet on the wall. Are you following me? Now, just...PLUG IN AND CHARGE UP—DAILY!

Today's Prayer:

Lord, You tell us in Psalm 29:11 that You are the source of our strength and You are the one who blesses us with peace. If there are areas in my life where I'm trying to do things on my own strength, will You bring them to mind? When I start to feel overworked, depressed, discouraged, or apathetic, remind me that I need to plug in to You and get recharged. Help me to stop seeing my life as a DIY project and instead, look to You as the source of my strength. In Jesus' name, I pray, AMEN.

PSALMS 31:1-2

Day 24:
Wisdom for Stepping Out in Faith

"O Lord, I have come to You for protection; don't let me be disgraced. Save me, for You do what is right. Turn Your ear to listen to me; rescue me quickly. Be my rock of protection, a fortress where I will be safe."
Psalms 31:1-2 (NLT)

Have you ever been in this situation? You've made a big commitment, or you've taken a step of faith and did something you were scared to do, and then your mind becomes flooded with thoughts like…Did I do the right thing? What if I can't do it? What if I fail and embarrass myself? What if people don't agree with what I am doing and criticize me?

These are all the thoughts and feelings that I felt before I launched a big project in my business recently. In fact, these thoughts delayed the launch for several weeks. But I have been taught that we are to move forward in spite of our fears.

The pastor at my church has told us that he was scared to death every time he was about to take a big step of faith, but he did it anyway. You might recognize him; his name is Rick Warren. He wrote *The Purpose Driven Church* and *The Purpose Driven Life* books.

I figured that if he moved forward in spite of his fears, I could too, so I went ahead and moved forward with launching my big project in spite of my fears, and so should you!

Psalms 31:1-2 is a great prayer if you know God is calling you to do something, but you're too afraid to take the first step. Know that God will protect you. If your honest, heartfelt desire is to do what He wants, then He will not let you be disgraced. He knows your heart. There's a popular acrostic for fear that is often so true!

***Fear** = **F**(alse) **E**(vidence) **A**(ppearing) **R**(eal)*

Go ahead…be bold. Do what you know God is telling you to do today!

Today's Prayer:

Lord, I know You want me to (fill in the blank). I'm really afraid of (fill in the blank). Please help me to move forward in spite of my fears. Help me to take a step of faith. I pray Psalm 31:1-2. I have come to You for protection; Lord, don't let me be disgraced. Save me, for You do what is right. Turn Your ear to listen to me; rescue me quickly. Be my rock of protection, a fortress where I will be safe. In Jesus' name, I pray, AMEN.

PSALM 31:3

Day 25:
Wisdom for Being a Good Follower

"Since You are my rock and my fortress, for the sake of Your name lead and guide me."
Psalm 31:3 NIV

David's boldness in this verse is crazy! Let me explain. When David prayed "...for the sake of your name," he was basically saying, "Lord, lead and guide me so that I don't mess up Your good name in front all these people watching." Now that is pretty darn bold, if you ask me. It's like saying "Even if I don't deserve it, God, help me out so Your reputation isn't tarnished."

We can pray to God in the same way. We can go to God and ask for Him to lead and guide us not because we deserve it, because we don't, but for His name's sake.

Where do you need guidance? I said it yesterday, and I'll say it again today –be bold! David was. Go to God and ask for Him to lead and guide you. When you do, keep two important things in mind:

1. Remember that when He's leading, you're following, not the other way around.

I grew up on a farm. When I got my horse to go riding, I used what you call a "lead rope." I hooked it onto her halter and led her over to the barn where the saddle was. As I led her over to the barn, I walked in front, and she followed me. Unfortunately, the same is not true when I walk my miniature Schnauzer, but I won't go into that story right now. The point is when God leads, He's in front, and you're following Him.

2. When God's guiding, you're listening, not the other way around.

Have you ever been on a guided tour somewhere? A while back, we took our daughter to visit a college campus. Part of the visit included a guided tour. The student who led the tour provided important highlights about each stop on the tour. We all walked together, but he did most of the talking while we listened. The same should be true when you ask for God's guidance. To get God's guidance, you need to tune in and listen. He should be doing most of the talking while you should be doing most of the listening.

Be bold in your prayer time today. It's okay if you don't feel adequate or deserving. Because God is your rock and your fortress, if for no other reason than for the sake of God's name, ask for Him to lead you and guide you!

Today's Prayer:

Lord, because You are my rock and my fortress, for the sake of Your name, lead and guide me. I know I'm bound to fail at (fill in the blank) if You don't help me, so please lead me and guide me. Show me any area where You're guiding but I'm not listening or where you're leading but I have stopped following. In Jesus' name, I pray, AMEN.

PSALMS 31:19-20

Day 26:
Wisdom for When a Situation is Out of My Control

"How great is the goodness You have stored up for those who fear You. You lavish it on those who come to You for protection, blessing them before the watching world. You hide them in the shelter of Your presence, safe from those who conspire against them. You shelter them in Your presence, far from accusing tongues."
Psalms 31:19-20 (NLT)

Have you ever found yourself in a situation where you see something that desperately needs to be addressed and changed, but no one else seems concerned? What's worse is that you have no power or authority to change the situation.

Verses 19 and 20 in Psalm 31 are powerful promises from our God who, unlike us, DOES have the power to change the situation.

However, did you notice that nowhere in these two verses does it say He will stop *those who conspire* against you or stop *the accusing tongues*.

What He does promise are these three things:

1. Lavish goodness on us who fear Him and go to Him for protection

2. Bless us before the watching world

3. Hide us in a safe shelter, far from the accusing tongues and those who conspire against us

I do not know what you're facing this week, but I myself have certainly faced some really challenging situations recently. To be honest, I spent a good hour one morning in tears crying out to God in sheer frustration and anguish over this one particularly difficult challenge. When I read this verse the very next morning, it could not have been better timing!

What are you facing this week? Have you been brought to tears over a situation that is out of your control? Are you stuck in a situation where any hope of change seems highly unlikely? Do what I did.

Go to God and cry out to Him for help. Ask Him to show you what you should do, if anything, and then DO IT.

Remember that He promises to lavish goodness on you when you go to Him for protection, bless you before the watching world, and hide you in a safe shelter from those who conspire against you!

Today's Prayer:

Lord, I feel very hopeless about (fill in the blank). I have no control over this situation, but I know You do. I'm just going to trust that You know what You're doing and stand on Your promise to me in Psalm 31:19-20 that You have stored up goodness for me when I show reverence and come to You for protection. And You will bless me before the watching world. I trust that no matter what happens with this situation, You will hide me in the shelter of Your presence, safe from those who conspire against me, far from accusing tongues. In Jesus' name, I pray, AMEN.

PSALM 32:8

Day 27: Wisdom for Saying "Yes" to God's Best

"The Lord says, 'I will guide you along the best pathway for your life. I will advise you and watch over you.' "
Psalm 32:8 (NLT)

If God says He will guide us along the *best* pathway for our lives, why then does it sometimes feel like the path we're on is riddled with hardships and hurdles? There are several legitimate reasons for these problems, but the main one is because God's definition of the word "best" does not include the word "easy". We automatically think we must have gotten off track if we're experiencing trouble. Not always.

Sometimes, the hardship is precisely what we need in order to mature and grow strong. A perfect example is when the butterfly goes through the struggle of breaking out of the cocoon. Did you know that if it does not use its legs and wings to break through the hard shell, it will not be strong enough to fly? The physical act of breaking through the shell strengthens the butterfly's wings and legs enabling it to fly once it's out of the cocoon. For a butterfly, being physically unable to fly poses a much bigger problem. Have you ever seen a butterfly walking around on the ground? Me neither. The only ones I've seen on the ground are DEAD ones.

If I were God and was guiding the little butterfly along the best pathway for his life; I would gladly say; "Get busy breaking through that shell. I know it's doesn't seem very fair that the first thing you have to face in your new little butterfly life is really hard and painful, but *trust* me; the alternative will not end well. So, if you want to fly, you must first break through that shell and, yes, you must do it by yourself. I will be here to cheer you on but I cannot do it for you."

God does the same in our lives. He may allow us to go through some immensely difficult circumstances so that we can develop a specific character trait we will need down the road. Because we can't see the future, we don't understand the necessity of our current challenge. We are often so eager to ask for great things from God, yet when He starts preparing us for those great things, we whine and cry about how hard the struggle is to get them.

It's like when I want to lose weight. I really want to lose the weight, but I hate working out and getting all sweaty. We want results without hard work. A while back, I was praying for God to help me reach a huge goal. I told Him about how difficult things were, and if He would help me reach this goal, it would be such a blessing. He calmly responded, "Yes, it will be a huge blessing, but it comes with even greater challenges than what you're facing right now. Do you still want it?"

Know that God wants to guide you along the best pathway for your life, but remember that it's not always going to be easy. In fact, in many ways, the best pathway for your life will include even greater challenges than the ones you're going through right now. The question is: how badly do you want God's best?

Today's Prayer:

Lord, Psalm 32:8 promises that You will guide me along the best pathway for my life. You promise to advise me and watch over me. If the challenge or circumstance I'm going through right now is preparing me to handle successfully the blessing You're going to bring down the road, help me to persevere. Give me the strength I need and teach me what I must learn until You feel I'm ready for the next step. Lord, I say yes! I do want Your best because I know it will be totally awesome. Even though the blessing may bring even greater challenges, I'm going to trust You to advise me and watch over me every step of the way! In Jesus' name, I pray, AMEN.

PSALMS 33:18-19

Day 28: Wisdom for Getting Through Times of Famine

"But the Lord watches over those who fear Him, those who rely on His unfailing love. He rescues them from death and keeps them alive in times of famine."
Psalms 33:18-19 (NLT)

Maybe you're not experiencing a real famine like the kind we hear about in other countries. But are you experiencing a relational famine caused by a conflict with your husband, a child, or friend? Are you experiencing a financial famine because of a lost job and mounting debt? If so, listen carefully.

Psalm 33:18 says the Lord will watch over you if you fear Him and rely on His unfailing love. Really? Yep. Fearing Him simply means showing awe and reverence. Part of showing reverence for others is placing a high value on what they say. Therefore, fearing God means valuing what He says to do.

Verse 19 tells us to rely on His unfailing love. Notice that it does not say to rely on our husband's love, our kids' love, or a friend's love for us. We must rely on God's unfailing love because His is the only kind that is UNFAILING. Human love fails.

Do you want to be rescued from the famine you're experiencing right now? Do these two things:

> **1. Make God's word a top priority and the main authority in your life.** Like I said, showing reverence for God means placing a high value on what He says and accepting His word as your authority. Simply put: read it and then do it.

> **2. Stop relying on the love of others that will greatly disappoint.** Refocus on God's unfailing love for you. How? Spend time with Him.

If you do what I suggest, you will not be disappointed. What have you got to lose? If things aren't going well the way you've been managing life, try something different. Don't wait for a famine to hit.

Today's Prayer:

Lord, You promise to watch over those who fear You and rely on Your unfailing love. You will rescue them from death and keep them alive in times of famine. I am going to make reading Your word a priority every day and accept it as the authority in my life. Help me to remember to rely solely on Your unfailing love. In Jesus' name, I pray, AMEN.

PSALM 34:4

Day 29:
Wisdom for Overcoming Fearful Thoughts

"I prayed to the Lord, and He answered me. He freed me from all my fears."
Psalm 34:4 (NLT)

Sometimes, I think that we forget to go to God first with our fears. If you're like me, you talk to yourself first. I usually get all stressed out by going over and over the issue in my mind. Then I talk to others to get their "take" on it. Then I talk to myself some more until I'm all worked up into a tizzy. Finally, the next morning during my prayer time with God; I pray to Him about it. By that time, I've usually lost a whole night of sleep over it. After praying to God about the issue, my fears and concerns begin to shrink.

Sound familiar? If we would just remember to go straight to God first, it would save us a lot of grief, worry, and consumption of Rolaids. Psalm 34:4 tells us to go to Him and He will answer us, but the hard part is remembering to go to God right when the problem initially pops up. Well, I'm going to suggest you try something that has helped me a lot.

Picture Jesus right next to you all day long. Track with me for a minute. Imagine that He's sitting next to you while you're putting on your makeup in the morning. Imagine that He is in the car with you on your way to work. Imagine He is sitting beside you at your desk reading email with you at work.

Imagine He's in the car with you on your way home. Do not, however, try explaining to the police officer when you get pulled over for being in the carpool lane that Jesus is in the car with you. Word of caution: it's possible that he might not appreciate your explanation.

At home, imagine He's beside you while you're frantically searching through the freezer hunting for something to make for dinner. Maybe I'm the only one who does that, but you get the idea.

Here's the crazy part, you're not really imagining anything. HE IS RIGHT BESIDE you all day long! In fact, if you are a believer, meaning you've asked Jesus to come into your heart, His Spirit dwells inside of you. He is seeing and hearing everything you are, including your thoughts.

When something pops up that stirs up fear or frustration, you can talk to Him in your thoughts. Isn't that awesome? You could be right in the middle of a heated conversation with someone and ask for help at that very same moment.

So today, what fears are swirling around in your head right now? Write everything you can think of in your journal. List every single concern. Now write down Psalm 34:4 in your journal. Make it a goal to memorize this verse so the next time a fearful thought looks for an opportunity to take up residency in your mind, you can recite Psalm 34:4.

Don't let those fearful thoughts rob another day. Start talking to God about it immediately. He's waiting to free you from your fear.

Today's Prayer:

Lord, I pray to You right now asking You to remove fearful thoughts of (fill in the blank) from my mind. I ask You to free me from these fears. When fearful thoughts start to plague my mind, help me to feel Your presence. Remind me that You are right beside me and promise to free me from all my fears when I ask. In Jesus' name, I pray, AMEN.

PSALMS 34:12-13

Day 30:
Wisdom for Choosing Helpful & Truthful Words

"Does anyone want to live a life that is long and prosperous? Then keep your tongue from speaking evil and your lips from telling lies!"
Psalms 34:12-13 (NLT)

This verse is pretty clear. Do you want to have a more successful business? Do you want to have better relationships? This verse promises success if we keep our tongue from speaking evil and our lips from telling lies. There are two questions to ask yourself before speaking.

Question 1- *Will what I'm about to say warm them up or burn them?*

James 3:5 (NLT) says, *"In the same way, the tongue is a small thing that makes grand speeches. But a tiny spark can set a great forest on fire."* Our tongues can either warm others or burn them.

Many times, when I'm in an argument with my husband, I know exactly which words I can use to set him off and which words will calm him down. The challenge is choosing the right ones. When I'm emotionally fired up, naturally, fire is the only thing that comes out of my mouth.

Here are two things that helped reduce this fire hazard in my home, they might just work for you, too:

> **1. Consciously take more time to respond in a heated conversation.** Instead of quickly responding to a statement with the first thing that comes to mind, pause and weigh possible responses in your head first. This helps you to remain calm and reduces the chance of saying something that will only fuel the fire. Personally, I've even been known to bite my lip in order to keep my mouth shut.
>
> **2. Intentionally take a time out when an argument has reached a boiling point.** This tends to be viewed as a big relief for my husband because I tend to be long winded, and the longer the argument lasts, the higher the odds it won't end well. Once you have a chance to cool down, you may realize the issue wasn't really worth arguing over.

Sometimes, you do need to reconvene at a later time to discuss the issue, but it's much easier to choose better words because you will have had time to cool down and think it over first.

Question 2- Am I telling the WHOLE truth?

Proverbs 14:25 (NIV) says, *"A truthful witness saves lives, but a false witness is deceitful."* It might not be that you're telling a bold-faced lie, but are you telling the *whole* truth? Are you leaving anything out in order to sway an outcome or avoid consequences?

Yep. I know. This one is a tough one to swallow. Our tongues are so small, yet they have so much power. However, if we want to live a life that is long and prosperous, we must not only keep our tongues from speaking evil, we must also keep our lips from telling lies.

Today's Prayer:

Lord, I definitely want to live a long and prosperous life, so I pray You will help me to keep my tongue from speaking evil and my lips from telling lies. When I'm about to choose the wrong words, stop me by reminding me of this verse. Help me to avoid the temptation to omit details to sway a decision or avoid consequences. In Jesus' name, I pray, AMEN.

PSALM 35:10

Day 31:
Wisdom for Defeating Hopelessness

"With every bone in my body I will praise Him: 'Lord, who can compare with You? Who else rescues the helpless from the strong? Who else protects the helpless and poor from those who rob them?' "
Psalm 35:10 (NLT)

If you're feeling defeated or hopeless today, I pray you will be encouraged as you read Psalm 35:10. David wrote this psalm when he was being chased—literally by an army that wanted to kill him. Yet, he praised God. Now that is gutsy. You may even think it sounds a little too unrealistic, but if you know what David had already been through up to this point, you wouldn't be so surprised his words. He knew God well. In fact, David had killed the giant Goliath, so he knew intimately the power available to protect him in his current predicament.

Do you know God that well to the point you can say, "With every bone in my body I will praise the Lord"? Even in the midst of a hopeless situation, could you speak as confidently as David did in this verse?

I'm here to tell you that you can! Whether you feel confident or not, the God who has saved your very life has no problem rescuing you from the strong! He has no problem protecting you from those who would rob you of your hope.

Reach out to God today with whatever has robbed you and say this verse as a praise to Him. Say it out loud. You heard me... Shout it out to the Lord! Repeat it as many times as it takes for your feelings to catch up with the TRUTH.

Write Psalm 35:10 in your journal. Then, write a list of things God has rescued or protected you from in the past. Finally, for the next few days, work on memorizing this verse. Whenever feelings of fear, defeat, or hopelessness creep in, say this verse over and over until those feelings go away.

Today's Prayer:

Lord, with every bone in my body I will praise you. Who can compare with you? Who else rescues the helpless from the strong? Who else protects the helpless and poor from those who rob them? Thank you Lord for rescuing me and protecting me from (fill in the blank). No matter what I may face today, I'm going to praise you because I know you will protect me from anyone and anything that threatens to rob me of my hope. In Jesus' name, I pray, AMEN.

ABOUT THE AUTHOR

Kristy Marcotte is a writer, speaker, and ministry leader. In 2008, she founded StraightTalkForWomen.com to help women strengthen their faith, family, and friendships. Her blog posts, podcasts, and videos, provide tips, tools, and God's truth for successful living. She and her husband have three children and live in Southern California.

For more information on how to connect with Kristy go to:
www.StraightTalkForWomen.com

I am so glad you decided to read *When I Pray*! If this book has helped you in any way, please let me know. I would love to hear from you.

When I Pray is part of a series I'm calling *31 Day Devotionals for Women*. So, if you enjoyed this first book, let me know and I will make sure you're in the loop when I get ready to publish the next book.

Visit

www.StraightTalkForWomen.com

To find out more about upcoming books in the

31 Day Devotionals for Women Series

When I Pray

When I Hope

When I Love

www.ingramcontent.com/pod-product-compliance
Lightning Source LLC
Chambersburg PA
CBHW070544300426
44113CB00011B/1781